BURRUNGUY
NOURLANGIE ROCK

A large composition of Binin (people) and mythic beings at the Anbangbang shelter, painted in 1964 by Najombolmi, known to Europeans as 'Barramundi Charlie'. This photograph was taken in 1979. Since then, further deterioration of the painted surfaces has occurred.

BURRUNGUY
NOURLANGIE ROCK

George Chaloupka

NORTHART

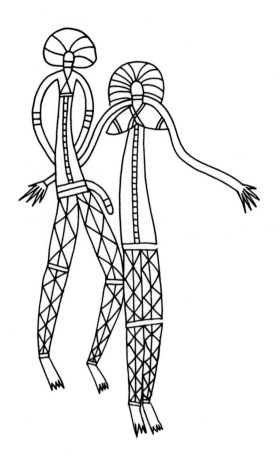

Front Cover:

Burrunguy Nourlangie Rock with the main escarpment of the Arnhem Land Plateau in the background.

Rock painting of Namandi, a malignant spirit in the Anbangbang shelter.

Back Cover:

Three catfish designs in the X-ray style, superimposed over earlier paintings. The fish in the centre of the panel shows a small crustacean in its gullet.

NORTHART

Burrunguy, also called Nourlangie Rock, is probably the best known as well as one of the most important features of the Kakadu National Park, which comprises of the western edge and the surrounding lowlands of the vast Arnhem Land Plateau. This area is a unique part of Australia and indeed of the world. The World Heritage Committee meeting in Sydney in October 1981 accepted the Australian Government's nomination for its inclusion on the register of World Heritage.

The prominent Burrunguy is the southernmost part of the Nourlangie Rock-Mt Brockman massif. Behind its imposing, brooding face lies a rugged interior with narrow crevices and gorges. Its structure has been revealed by the uplifting and tilting of the sandstone mass, exposing earlier rocks including conglomerates laid down at th beginnings of its formation. White quartz crystal veins crisscross rock surfaces in one of the gorges, and nodules of iron oxides are exposed on the floor of an upland basin. The sandstone has been greatly weathered, forming pillars and bridges that span residuals, and numerous walls have been undermined and have collapsed, forming shelters. Elsewhere, sheer cliffs of resistant sandstone rise steeply above the talus slopes, their variegated walls stained in colours which the Aborigines were to use in their paintings, the rocks brought into sharp relief by pockets of the large myrtaceous evergreen tree (*Allosyncarpia ternata*) unique to this region.

The animals living here, like the chestnut-quilled rock pigeon (*Petrophassa rufipennis*), are also of the earth colours, shy of man and blending into the landscape. It is only towards the end of the dry season that one can see the black walleroo (*Macropus bernardus*) and the Alligator River euro, two species frequently found as subjects in the rock paintings of the region, as they come from their rocky lairs to drink from springs emerging at the base of the escarpment.

The Arnhem Land Plateau, of which Burrunguy is a residual is the Northern Territory's major physiographic unit. It is like a large rocky island, with its western and northern edges — the escarpment rising steeply above the adjacent plains. The general elevation of the plateau varies from 250 to 300 metres, with higher residuals of rock reaching more than 500 metres, indicating its original height. The outliers of the plateau range from small residuals dotting the floodplains to large massifs such as Nourlangie Rock-Mt Brockman and delineate its former extent. European scientists say that this sandstone complex was laid down some 1600 million years ago after weathering of earlier formations, and indeed the ripple marks evident in the crossbedded layers of collapsed rocks confirm the deposition of sands that in time were metamorphosed into sandstone and orthoquartzites. Later the complex itself became subject to weathering: the creeks and rivers flowing across the plateau cut deep gorges and valleys where joints and faultlines weakened the formation, and numerous waterholes and waterfalls were formed. Weathering also sculpted the present residuals and caused collapsing of rock and the formation of protective overhangs which in time were used by Aborigines as occupational shelters.

Aboriginal people colonised this region soon after landing on the greater Australian continent some 50 000 years ago, during one of the Ice Ages. At this time the sea was much lower than at present and a landbridge connected Australia with New Guinea, while exposed continental shelves extended towards the present-day islands of Indonesia. The Aborigines say that they have always lived here, and that the features of landscape as well as the people were created long ago by their ancestors, during the creation period of Dreaming. It was their ancestral beings — not mere physical forces — who shaped the land, sent out the spirit beings to populate the land, and then taught the people traditions which they follow to this day. The creative beings' presence permeates the landscape of Kakadu now, as it once did the whole of Australia.

The mid-sector of the western part of the Arnhem Land Plateau is drained by three streams that in the lowlands, flowing past Burrunguy, become the many braided Nourlangie Creek before it floods out into the wetlands. During the dry season the waters recede and the vast wetlands shrink into several waterholes where tens of thousands of magpie geese (*Anseranus semipalmata*) and whistle ducks (*Dendrocygna arcuata)* congregate, before the next wet season rains raise the creeks to flood the plains again.

The first Europeans to visit this region were Ludwig Leichhardt and the members of his party of exploration. In 1845, towards the end of their epic journey from Moreton Bay in Queensland to Victoria Settlement in Port Essington on the Cobourg Peninsula, the party had crossed the rugged Arnhem Land Plateau and followed the Jim Jim Creek to where, on the edge of the plains, it joined the South Alligator River. Vast, seemingly impenetrable wetlands opened before them. Skirting these swamps and following the higher ground, they came across a well beaten path that led them to a group of Aborigines. Leichhardt in his journal called them 'our good friends the natives' and mentions that they were already well acquainted with the effect of firearms. The Aborigines, friendly and inquisitive, carrying bundles of goose spears and spearthrowers, flocked to their camp from every direction. As they guided Leichhardt's party safely across the wetlands, they showed their skill in spearing geese.

The next Europeans to visit the area passed between the Nourlangie Rock-Mt Brockman massif and the main escarpment in 1865. They were McKinley and his party of exploration, who were sent by the South Australian Government to seek a new "capital" for their Northern Territory, for the first settlement of Escape Cliffs at the mouth of the Adelaide River had proved unsuitable for the government's plans of developing the north. The party's journals describe the failure of their journey, the tension, arguments and fears as they faced the flooded countryside and the forbidding stone country. After five long months they reached the banks of the East Alligator River, only 200 kilometres east of their point of departure.

Even then they were not sure where they were as McKinley thought they had discovered a new river and attempted to call it Alexandrina. There they killed their remaining horses and used the hides to cover a punt-like craft in which they miraculously sailed and drifted down the river and along the coast back to Escape Cliffs. Their tales of inhospitable country and of the Aborigines contrasted with those given by Leichhardt, but this can be partly accounted for by the difference between the dry and wet seasons, and by man's abilities and attitudes.

The imposing face of Burrunguy Nourlangie Rock rises steeply from the lowlands. The massive rockfall at its base was used as a wet season shelter by the Warramal people.

In the 1880s buffalo shooters had moved into the region to exploit the large numbers of buffaloes that by then spread from Cobourg Peninsula across the Alligator River Plains. These animals had been brought to the country to provide a reliable meat supply for the two earliest settlements on the northern coast, Fort Wellington and Victoria. Some escaped and others were released when the settlements were abandoned. Leichhardt came across the earliest of these buffaloes in 1845 in the vicinity of present-day Oenpelli.

▲ *Namargon, the Lightning Man. The band encircling his body represents the lightning, while the stone axes protruding from his head and others attached to his knees and elbows are used during the wet season to strike the clouds and release the lightning.*

▶ *Namargon djadjan, Lightning Dreaming, a sacred-dangerous site whose disturbance could cause harm to all the people living in the region. Namargon, the Lightning Man, came here from his place of origin in the interior of the Arnhem Land Plateau and his movement delineates the extent of the Rol clan's territory.*

The two family groups painted at the Anbangbang shelter by Najombolmi. The Binin and Dalug men and women are portrayed in the X-ray style with stylised rayed hair and breast girdles. Two of the women are depicted with milk in their breasts. Water seeping from rock fissures above runs over the painted surfaces, obliterating some of the paintings.

The buffalo shooters shot the animals for their hide. Their first camps were on the high ground near the river banks, where boats could land to bring in supplies and to load the cargo. One such camp was on the South Alligator River at Kapalgu, some distance downstream of the present bridge site.

Shooting of buffaloes, transport and processing of hides proved to be a labour-intensive industry. The source of cheap available labour was the Aborigines who lived in the region. At Kapalgu more than 100 people worked for the early entrepeneurs. As more shooters established their camps between the Alligator Rivers, the buffalo population on the plains decreased and the hunting parties were forced to move upstream towards the escarpment and into the escarpment valleys, areas previously not exploited. An additional advantage of this move inland was that the shooting of buffaloes could commence there earlier in the year, at the time when the plains were still too wet. Along the way they established a number of staging camps. One such camp was on the banks of a deep waterhole surrounded by paperbark trees and encircled by residual rocks. A sandy bank sloped into cool, sweet water where the giant perch, barramundi (*Lates calcarifer*) were plentiful and where people could wash off the dust of the journey.

They had to be careful though, as the large saltwater crocodiles also made their home here, a long way from the river estuaries where they are usually found. Their tracks and the impressions of their bodies were on the sandbanks where they sunned themselves and also in the muddy channel which led to an upstream waterhole.

This camp was even more appreciated by the Aboriginal members of the shooting parties, many of whom were traditional owners of this or surrounding parts of the land. They knew the area intimately, for they had often camped with their families in the nearby shelters, speared fish in the waterholes and hunted walleroos and wallabies in the rocks. To them this place was Nawulandja, and from the top of the residuals rising above the waterhole they pointed out other features of the surrounding landscape. Above the open grassy flat, in the midst of which was a large shallow waterhole, its surface reflecting the pale trunks of the paperbark trees, rose the imposing rock Burrunguy. From behind it emerged the sheer wall of the escarpment that continued, seemingly uninterrupted, till it merged with the horizon far to the south. Escarpment gorges and valley openings lay across it as blue shadows. One of these was Namargon djadjan, where the fluted rocks represented the dangerous site of the Lightning Man; others were Yelegabuju, Yuwendelu and Balawuru, the last a valley, the source of Deaf Adder Creek. From the open forest to the south-west rose a conical hill called Bupa. The Aborigines also named landscape features and localities which the Europeans could not discern. They were waterholes, creeks, campsites, sacred and dreaming sites, and their "countries". One dreaming site which the Europeans could see and were to visit was Guluban djang, meaning Flying Fox Dreaming, and also its increase centre. This was situated in the vicinity of Dabul, a waterhole completely surrounded by a deep green belt of pandanus palms and paperbark trees, where several colonies of black flying foxes made their home. The Europeans did not remember all the names they were told or the features which those represented. Burrunguy, the imposing rock, became Nourlangie as that was how they recalled the name Nawulandja.

An unusual depiction of Namargon, the Lightning Man, portrayed in skeletal form with only half his body. His large phallus superimposes an earlier painting of a man carrying a number of dilly bags.

A rock painting of the seldom portrayed Barginj, the wife of Namargon, the Lightning Man.

For many years buffalo shooters and the odd prospector were the only Europeans to visit this region. Aborigines continued to live in their land, mainly during the wet season when the buffalo shooters closed their camps and returned to town. They followed a traditional way of life, hunting and visiting the important sites of their land where they carried out the appropriate rituals. Within the shelters they recorded in vivid images the activities of Europeans, their possessions and the animals that they introduced. During this period they also brought back burial parcels containing skeletons of those who died while working away from their homeland.

During the 1960s several safari operators established themselves in the region. The tourist flew in by small aircraft, then transferred to four-wheel drive vehicles and ventured to places where previously only a man on a horse could get. The safari operators 'scrub-bashed' a track to the three areas which are now open to the public. The original track led first to Nangaluwur, a large occupational and rock painting site on the northern side of the massif. From there it followed the rocks to Burrunguy (*Nourlangie Rock*) and the Angangbang site, and then led across the flat to Nawulandja waterhole and rocks, a location which they have named Little Nourlangie. In 1962 these sites were visited by David Attenborough, the English naturalist, who was the first to record the rock paintings found within the shelters on film and in book. However, it was after his visit that the major frieze of spirit beings and people at Anbangbang was executed. Since then, with the continuous development taking place in the region and the concomitant improvement of vehicular access, Nourlangie Rock sites have been seen by thousands of visitors and the rock paintings which they have admired are now seen in films, magazines and books all around the world. This visitation has further increased since the establishment of the Kakadu National Park.

Burrunguy, Nangaluwurr, Nawulandja and Dabul are four main sites in the core territory of the Warramal clan of the Gundjeitmi-speaking people. Further along the Nourlangie Rock-Mt Brockman massif lived the Kodjkarndi, whilst the escarpment of the plateau and some distance into its interior was the traditional land of the Rol and Badmardi clans. Downstream along the Nourlangie Creek lived the clans of the Ambukala and Bukunejtja language groups who shared with them the bounty of the wetland resources.

Members of a given clan are spiritually linked to a specific territory which encompasses a number of features and sites where the mythic beings, during the creation period of the Dreaming, performed a certain act, left a part of themselves, or remained at the end of that period. Within each clan's territory there is at least one site which represents the life essence of a particular species. The traditional owners of the land carry out appropriate rituals at each of these centres which ensure the distribution of the species across the land. Thus, the Warramal were responsible for Guluban djang which contains the life essence of the black flying fox (*Pteroptus alecto*). They enacted their ritual at this site and called out names of locales and territories where this species should prosper. The clans were inter-dependent and sharing communities. They hunted and collected food and resources over one another's territory, sharing the seasonal bounty of a particular area. Through their travels they knew intimately large areas of land, their spiritual bases, the dreamings and the sacred and dangerous sites, and in their presence behaved accordingly.

Members of more distant clans, even those who spoke different languages visited the Warramal territory frequently. Djauan-speaking clans from the headwaters of the South Alligator and Katherine rivers came across the plateau to participate in ceremonies, and also to partake of the resources of the wetlands when, towards the end of the dry season the magpie geese had retreated to the diminishing waterholes and were speared as they fed or were knocked down as they flew low overhead.

15

From the east came the representatives of Wunigag, Erre and even Kunwinjggu, who stopped to camp at Dabul or Nawulandja before continuing on their way to the South Alligator River where it flows through the Ambukala land. The river there is fringed by thick stands of bamboo, and it was this resource, not obtainable in their own lands, that these visitors came to collect. They cut the young stems for the shafts of their spears and carried bundles of them back to their homelands. The visitors were always welcome, for they brought news and gossip, told stories, and in song and dance described activities of mythic beings and spirit people inhabiting their lands. Occasionally they also executed a painting on the wall of a shelter which they shared.

Perhaps the most frequent visitors were the families of the Badmardi clan who were particularly close to Warramal. They said that they were of 'one river': a creek which originated in their valley was the main source of Nourlangie Creek. This clan also brought the remains of their dead to Burrunguy or Nawulandja for burial. The Badmardi always left their escarpment valley in the middle of the wet season and followed high ground to Nourlangie Rock, where for several days they stayed with the Warramal clan in the Angangbang shelters. From there both clans made their way to the flooded plains, where at that time of the year magpie geese made nests and laid eggs on the reedy platforms. Here, members of the local groups ventured on rafts into the wetlands, collecting only a few eggs from every nest, later to share them with their visitors in the bounty of the 'goose egg time'. After several weeks both clans returned to Nourlangie Rock, where the Badmardi, before leaving for their own land, camped at Nangaluwurr and Angangbang again. During the dry seasons the Warramal and also the Ambukala and the Bukunejtja clans from the wetlands would visit the Badmardi in their escarpment valley. They made their camp on the soft sandy banks of a stream where it emerged from a gorge. From there a string of deep waterholes led to a sacred waterfall. Here they all stayed, the men spearing fish and freshwater crocodiles whilst the women collected wild honey, until it was time to return to the wetlands to hunt the mature geese and file snakes (*Acrochordus arafurae*) and long-necked turtles (*Chelodina rugosa*). In the immediate vicinity of their camp, on both sides of the escarpment, were rock shelters where the men would go and fashion spearheads out of hard quartzite cores and discuss paintings that decorated the walls. Some of these they knew were executed in the Dreaming by the Mimi spirits, who taught the succeeding generations of people how to paint. Others were of mythic beings who 'put themselves' on the rock, their spiritual substance remaining within the image, whilst the more recent paintings were done by people, by members of Badmardi family groups.

Although nearly all the men at times executed a rock painting, some men were considered to be more skilful than others and their paintings were much admired. One such artist was Najombolmi of the Badmardi clan who painted numerous designs not only in his own land but also in the territories of the adjoining clans. Of these paintings his large frieze of humans and spirit figures at Nourlangie Rock is the most famous.

The paintings at Nourlangie Rock form only a small, though unique, segment of rock art treasures of Kakadu and of the other regions of the Arnhem Land Plateau.

Hand stencils and small running figures of an early rock painting style cover the ceiling of this high overhang in the Nangaluwurr shelter.

▲
A series of 'blue paintings', similar in design to the figures at Anbangbang shelter and also painted by Najombolmi. The blue pigment is the European washing blue, a colour which held some fascination for the Aboriginal artists.

▶
Rock painting of the Fly River turtle, which until recently was known only from the rivers of southern New Guinea. After this painting was recognised to represent this species, several specimens of the turtle were collected in Northern Territory rivers. This is one of the 'blue paintings' from a shelter located near the Nawulandja waterhole.

The first such impressions were painted perhaps 20,000 or more years ago, and this tradition has continued uninterrupted to the present, with the last known rock painting being executed in 1972. From the very beginning it was a naturalistic art which depicted recognizable changes in people's physical, social and cultural environment. Indeed, the prehistory of their land, as well as the more recent events commencing with the first European contact, are illustrated here in thousands of vivid images.

The sequence of these developments and changes is revealed in identifiable rock art styles superimposed over each other, and suggested by the presence or absence of certain subjects. There are paintings of long extinct animals and of others introduced into the region when sea levels rose at the end of the last Ice Age. New types of spear are shown in some styles, while others depict weapons that are no longer used. Mythic beings appear alongside man, and often very old groups of figures portrayed in vivid action have been superimposed by large, still figures painted much later.

Rock paintings of hands and arms such as these belong to the recent horizon of rock art.

The pigments used were of the earth: red and yellow ochre of many hues, white pipeclay or the rare white mineral huntite, black as charcoal or manganese oxide. Later, after the European contact, a blue pigment the newcomers' 'washing blue' was also used. The wet pigments, prepared on a stone pallete by rubbing in water, was applied to the rock surface with brushes made of human hair, fibrous stalks or feathers, the last being used to produce the fine sinuous lines of the early figures and the intricate cross hatching in the more recent designs. Larger areas were smeared on by hand and occasionally paint held in the mouth was 'blown' on to further decorate a painting. This technique was also used when making stencils of hands and objects such as boomerangs. Dry pigment pieces of ochre held as a chalk to draw with were seldom used. Perhaps the first images of this region's rock art were the handprints achieved by wetting the palm of the hand with red pigment and pressing it against the rock face. Similarly, heads and stalks of grasses were covered with wet pigment and then struck against the rock.

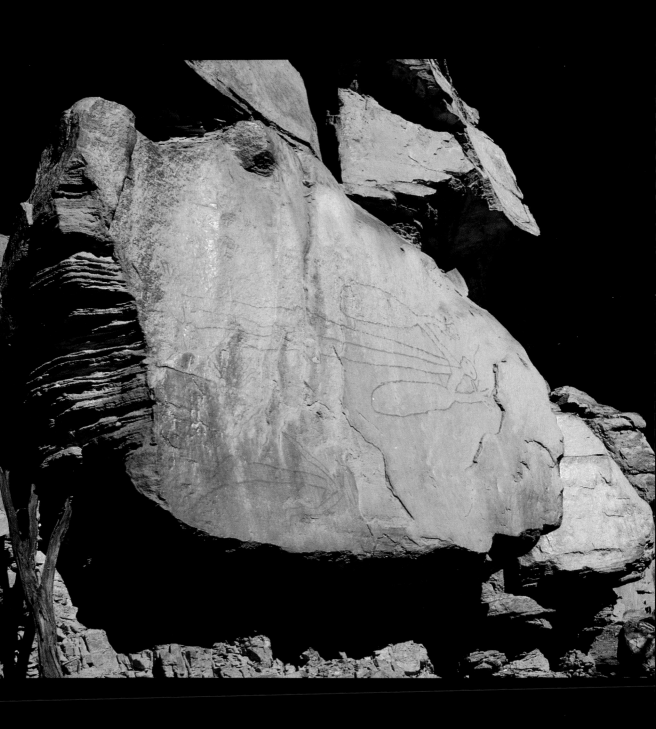

Namandi spirit and its companion, on a rock face fully exposed to sun and rain. The dilly bags hanging from the malignant spirit's arm were intended for the victim's heart, liver, lungs and kidneys.

A group of female spirit figures, superimposed over earlier paintings. The small figure with four arms is Alkajiko, an associate of Namargon, the Lightning Man.

In the past, Europeans have simply divided the rock art of this region into two styles - the very old Mimi and the more recent X-ray. Mimi are said to be spirit people who were the first to paint and who taught this skill to the Aborigines. The Aborigines now describe any painting which is of some antiquity, in styles other than they have used in their designs as being the work of those spirit people. Actually there is a number of recognisable styles before the commencement of the X-ray style. Some of these styles depict large animals and human beings, others show groups of people in narrative scenes. Exquisite drawings of men in hunt, conflict or a ceremony, are followed by a style in which human beings are simplified to a stick-like form. During some periods, more than one style was used at the same time. However, it is the most recent style of large multicoloured X-ray figures which is perhaps the best known. In this style of intellectual realism, the artist portrayed not only the subject's external shape but also its internal configuration. Human and animal figures are shown with anatomical features and internal organs, while inanimate objects such as a rifle may be depicted with a bullet in its breach. This style is well represented in the rock shelters of the Nourlangie Rock massif.

The best known of the Nourlangie Rock shelters is Angangbang, approached via a pathway from a parking area some 900 metres away. It lies at the base of the massif and is formed by large boulders and rocks that have fallen from the terraces and cliff faces above. From within, spirit beings and human figures look over the adjacent clearing. When David Attenborough visited this site, he saw weathered images of similar figures and also other subjects, all of which are now superimposed by later paintings. During his visit he found the floor of this shelter covered with long sheets of bark laid over saplings, forming a platform that in turn was covered by a thick layer of paperbark - the remnants of a mattress, blanket and a pillow. Grinding hollows in the outcropping rock and portable mortars still held the pebble shaped pestles, while the ground was littered with stone scrapers, blades and used pieces of ochre. A remnant of a spearthrower and several sticks were firmly lodged in a rock fissure, providing hooks for Aborigines to hang their dilly bags. A cavern at the back of the shelter was a burial chamber with a number of burial parcels containing skeletons. Now only the rock paintings, considerably weathered again, and the grinding hollows in the rock remain.

It was in this shelter that Najombolmi, known to Europeans as Barramundi Charlie, executed perhaps his best painting. For many years he worked for Europeans as a buffalo shooter, in a gold mine and on cattle stations, returning to his land whenever he could. In 1964, only a year before his death, he camped for the last time in this shelter. By then he had witnessed the impact of European contact on the Aboriginal sociocultural systems elsewhere in the Northern Territory, and now he saw changes happening within his own region. Bridges began to span the rivers, which were the actual barriers in the past, and each year an increasing number of outsiders were

▲
Rock paintings of two female Namandi spirits with long nipples, toes and head protrusions.

◀
There are many portrayals of mythic beings within the Nangaluwurr shelter. Most are said to represent the Namandi spirits, including this figure with six-fingered hands and a long dilly bag.

intruding into his land. He thought of the people who once used to live here, and of the Dreaming. In his swag he carried ochres which he had collected on his travels. He took them out, prepared the pigments and painted the people back into the shelter. There are two family groups, men standing amidst their wives, some of whom he depicted with milk in their breast, as if he really wished them to be alive, to procreate and to people the land again. He built a platform and from this he painted the mythic beings, Namargon the Lightning Man and his wife Barginj, and Namandjolk, a malignant spirit. This painted wall is unique, the last work of a great artist. Yet this nation, which at great expense buys works of other cultures and builds mausoleums to house them, ignores the genius of its own land. Unprotected, not only from natural weathering but also from buffaloes which rub their bodies against the painted wall and from the fingers of curious visitors who cause the fragile pigment to flake, the lower half of this magnificent frieze is nearly defaced.

There are two other extensive shelters in the immediate vicinity of this main Angangbang gallery. The first is only fifty metres away, formed by a vaulted ceiling of an overhanging terrace. The rock here is conglomerate, consisting of large quartz pebbles embedded in sandstone, and because of its partly impermeable surface,

25

A dolphin-like painting, originally executed in red and white, in the western part of the Nangaluwurr shelter.

paintings here weather rapidly. Nevertheless, there is a group of well preserved spirit figures near the ceiling, and further along the wall are hand stencils and paintings of guns and kangaroos. The occupational area of this site is enclosed by roof-fall rocks, its surfaces pitted with grinding hollows in which food items were prepared over millennia. Further out stand tall trees screening the site from the outside world. Only an indirect sun filters through the leaves and for most of the day a green light fills the shelter.

In the rains of the wet season a silver curtain of water envelopes this site. Years ago, before the intensive visitation began, the seldom seen black-banded alligator pigeon (*Ptilinopus cinctus*) nested in a tree whose branches reached into the shelter.

Further along the base of the massif is the largest shelter in the region, formed by a gigantic boulder that has fallen from the massif and lodged itself in the scree slope below. Its angled ceiling, resting on previously fallen rocks, is blackened by smoke from many a wet season campfire.

26

In April, at the beginning of the dry season people moved from the Nourlangie Rock sites to Nawulandja rocks and waterhole. They walked around the billabong, which during the wet season was flooded by Bandalg Creek and by backwater from Nourlangie Creek. The excess water drained back towards the creek through a narrow connecting channel and the people paused here to spear fish struggling through the channel, disturbing a pair of white breasted sea eagles (*Heliaetus leucogaster*) that also fished here, taking the fish to their nearby nest. Further downstream, egrets, herons, spoonbills, and long-legged jabirus were wading, picking out the passing fish.

A passageway between rock residuals leads from the plain to the waterhole. Just to the north, a crevice in the steep, sloping terraced rock was cut in the Dreamtime by Badbong, the rock wallaby (*Petrogale lateralis*). The shaded pool at its base has crystal clear water with blue waterlilies floating on its surface and it provided fresh water well into the dry season. Beyond the entrance gap, the rocks open to reveal a park-like setting where weathered conglomerate boulders, their white quartz pebbles standing out against the dark-stained sandstone, stand like sculptured pieces. Underneath one such rock, an overhang that faces the track forms a small shelter. This is the site of the 'blue paintings', where the artist Najombolmi experimented with a new, exotic pigment.

The depicted human figures are executed in the traditional manner, using the techniques and conventions of the X-ray style. But the most interesting painting is that of a turtle. It depicts the Fly River turtle (*Carettochelys insculpta*) which until recently was thought to be endemic to New Guinea, and it was only after this painting had been identified as representing this species, that several specimens of the turtle were collected in Northern Territory rivers. Although these are the best known paintings with blue pigment, other artists were also fascinated by this colour, and designs where the pigment was used are found throughout the escarpment.

Near the Nawulandja waterhole is a long, low boulder. On its western side, facing the waterhole, are two niches which until 1970 contained several burial parcels. Before that time the only disturbance to their contents was by a theatrically inclined European, who had placed skulls into crossed bones so that they stood out starkly against the dark background, watching over their land. On the other side of this rock is a low overhang where people sheltered at the beginning and towards the end of the wet season. This site was excavated in 1973 and the contents document its Aboriginal use over the past 10,000 years. Used pieces of ochre, stone tools and remnants of bone and shell suggest their activities. They speared the fish and water birds, and hunted the rock wallaroos, rock wallabies, possums, bandicoots, native cats and water rats, as well as smaller marsupials. The shells of freshwater mussels were found only in the upper layer of the deposit, implying a recent introduction into this area.

On the northern side of the Nourlangie Rock Massif is Nangaluwurr, a large and important rock painting and occupational site. The shelter follows the base contours of a high cliff, where it meets the scree slope. Its floor, except for the mid section where occupational deposits and rocks with grinding hollows delineate the living area, is on many levels. It varies in width and runs out over the rocks to the extremities of the shelter. The rock surface, although of hard and mostly smooth sandstone, is

A fully rigged sailing ship, trailing an anchor and pulling a dinghy, which may have been one that brought provisions to the buffalo shooters' camp at Kapalgu on the South Alligator River.

jointed and fractured and weathers along the bedding planes. The paintings in this shelter extend intermittently over a distance of 200 metres and are situated from ground level to a ceiling of eight-metre high overhangs. Many of the ledges on which the early artists stood to paint such designs have since collapsed and perhaps cover the original occupational deposits. This may explain why the charcoal sample from the first finds found at the lowest levels of an archaeological excavation here was only some 800 years old, when the rock painting styles found in the shelter suggests a much earlier visitation and use of this site.

Most of the rock art styles of the region, some in unique examples, are represented at Nangaluwurr. Underneath a high overhang are small running figures in large head-dresses, carrying boomerangs and spears. The figures are surrounded by hand stencils, some of which are of the three middle fingers closed tightly together with extending little finger and thumb. At eye level below, are painted outlines of hands and forearms, while nearby on a projecting rock exposed to the elements is an outline painting of a Namandi spirit with long dilly bags hanging from his arms. There are other mythic figures further along the wall, including male and female Namandi, and Alkajko - a female spirit with four arms and horn-like protuberances. One unusual figure is of a dolphin-like creature executed in a bright red pigment.

On the wall above the occupational deposit in the middle of the shelter sails a two-mastered ship, trailing an anchor chain in the water and with a dinghy floating behind. Nearby is a group of paintings, the work of Najombolmi's friend "Old Nym" Djimogor, a Wardjag man who came into this region from Arnhem Land many years before. Executed at approximately the same time as Najombolmi's paintings at Anbangang, it is a frieze of fish and a short necked turtle. Old Nym had worked at first as a buffalo shooter and later cut cypress pine at Anlar, the site of the present day Nourlangie Ranger Station. Some time after he completed these paintings, a European visited the shelter and placed dieselene soaked rags in a rock fissure and set them alight in an attempt to destroy Djimogor's paintings. He was unsuccessful, but the paintings remain blackened by smoke, giving testimony of man's prejudice and insensitivity. The burial grounds also suffered at the hands of callous visitors. Many caverns, crevices, niches and shelters at Nourlangie Rock and Nawulundja were depositories of burial parcels for several local clans. The human remains were brought here in dilly bags or wrapped in paperbark. Later, sugar bags and sheets of canvas were also used. The early European visitors, buffalo shooters and safari operators who visited these sites accompanied by Aborigines respected such remains, as they had known some of the people interred here. However, the burials did not survive the influx of visitors who came in ever increasing numbers from the beginning of 1970. Whereas in the past, visitors were guided by the safari operators, they now came in their own vehicles.

In the neocolonial manner, in a four-wheel drive vehicle with an esky full of beer instead of a horse and canteen of water, they possessed the land and pillaged everything within it. Skeletal material, skulls as well as bones, and the accompanying 'swags' - dilly bags full of meaningful possessions of the deceased were taken.

One of these 'swags' was described by Allan Stewart, a well-known safari operator. Its contents consisted of a fighting dilly bag, a black egg-shaped stone, a finely painted message stick and a blue tobacco tin featuring a fully rigged sailing ship.

It is this well justified fear of further disturbance of their kin's remains, as well as the possibility of disturbance or even damage to the Dreaming and sacred sites of the region, that is the basic reason why the Aborigines are wary of unaccompanied and unchecked movement of Europeans through their land. They also seek consideration for the many groups of spirit people, such as the Mimi, Nukdjarang and Nagitjgitj, who they believe inhabit the stone country of the escarpment and the plateau.

◀ Rock paintings of a short-necked turtle, two barramundi and a black bream, painted by 'Old Nym' Djimogor and damaged by fire set by a European who wanted to destroy them.

▼ Most of the damage to rock paintings, with the exception of those in sites subject to intense visitation, is caused by natural agents such as water. To prevent this damage, an artificial dripline was placed on the edge of the overhang to divert water from flowing over the painted surfaces.

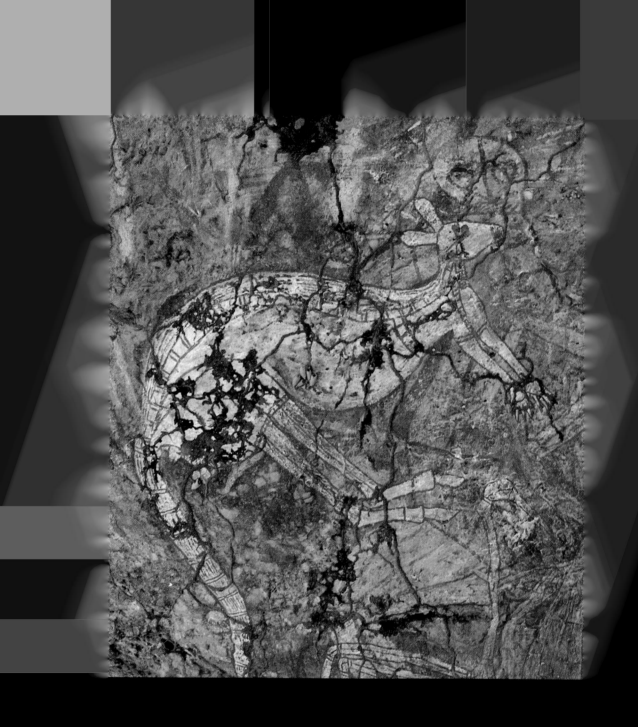

passages and wasp nests built over painted surfaces are a common cause of damage to
ntings, as can be seen in this example from one of the Anbangbang shelters.

ore a temporal sequence of rock art styles and their relative dating can be established, ind
es and their superimpositions must be identified. A series of paintings in this shelter sugg
uence with the hand prints as the earliest images, whilst the yellow figures of a spirit be

The last rock painting in their region was executed in the dry season of 1972, painted to commemorate a family group's journey, when the painter took his wife and his young children to 'show them the land'. On an exposed rockface of a weathered sculptured residual, in the shadow of which they camped, he painted white silhouettes of a kangaroo and a goanna. The next season's rains washed away this pigment and now not a trace of these paintings remains. Rock paintings once destroyed are irreplaceable. It is for this reason that protection of rock art sites and conservation of their painted surfaces is the most important task facing the National Park's Service. The rock shelters of Kakadu are open air museums and art galleries. Their preservation is a weighty responsibility, for these treasures are not only our heritage, but that of all mankind.

▲ *These small hunter figures, depicted in exaggerated movement, are shown wearing elaborate head-dresses with tassels, long pubic fringes or 'skirts' hanging from their waist belts, and carrying boomerangs and spears. This style of dynamic figure also belongs to an early horizon of rock art.*

◀ *Images of large animals and human beings belong to an early period of rock art, here represented by a kangaroo with a joey in its pouch.*

The rock paintings of Thylacines (Tasmanian tigers), animals which became extinct on the Australian mainland some 3,500 years ago, suggest rock art's antiquity. Elsewhere in the region, paintings of animals that may have become extinct 18,000 years ago point to an early development of this art form.

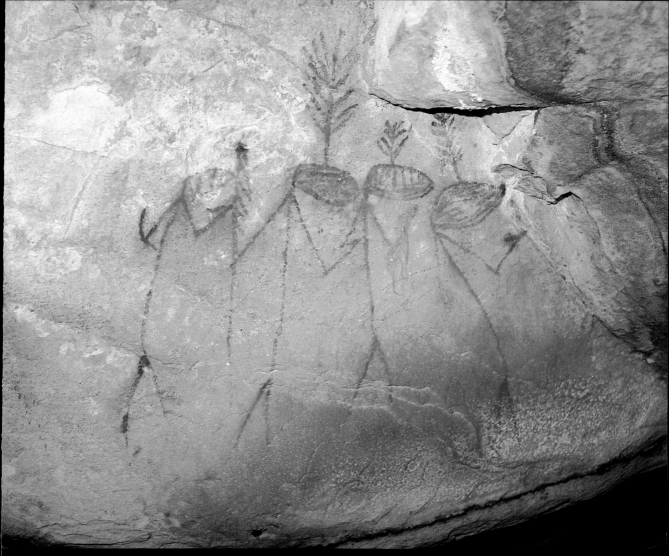

The simple figures, reduced to a stick-like form retain head-dresses and use boomerangs and spears of the preceding dynamic figures. However, a new weapon - a fighting pick - was introduced.

Rising sea levels at the end of the last Ice Age introduced estuarine fauna into the rivers of this region. Barramundi, the giant perch, was to become the dominant subject in the art of riverine populations.

In recent times, freshwater swamps and waterholes developed over the saline flats adjacent to estuarine rivers, and birds frequenting such wetlands first appeared in the rock art.

There are many unusual features to be found around the Nourlangie Rock massif, such as this natural stone bridge spanning weathered residuals, with the fragile whispy 'deviltrees' said to be the source of the Namandi spirits.